A Prairie Year

TEXT BY JO BANNATYNE-CUGNET

ART BY YVETTE MOORE

TUNDRA BOOKS

Introduction

Life on the prairies is governed by the seasons — spring, summer, fall and winter — and prairie folk take pride in adapting to each season's weather and temperatures. Children on the prairies take particular pleasure in these changing seasons. As we journey through the months of a prairie year, you may experience their sense of pleasure.

January is the month of tournaments on ice — curling, ringette and hockey. Quonset community rinks become beehives of activity. Weekends, our town streets can seem deserted. Everyone is either at the rink or out of town to a tournament. These same towns boast of producing world champion curlers and many NHL players — Gordie Howe, Bobby Clarke, Brian Trottier, Tiger Williams, the Sutter brothers, the list goes on.

February can seem the longest month, even though it has the least number of days. Short hours of sunshine mean getting on the school bus in the morning in darkness and coming home after school in darkness. Folks tire of the cold and snowstorms that often leave them housebound. You can end up with a case of "winter doldrums." The best cure for this is to go out for the weekend ice fishing, cross-country skiing or snowmobiling.

March is maternity month for livestock on the prairies. Farmers and ranchers arrange to have the birthing happen after the worst of winter is over and before they have to be out working on the land. They must be on hand, day or night, should any animals run into difficulties delivering their babies.

April is a month of waiting. We wait for the last bit of snow and ice to melt. The land lies cold and damp, so we wait for it to warm up. Sloughs and fields of bleached stubble provide a "bed and breakfast" for flocks of geese and ducks migrating to their northern summer homes. Their return is reassuring. We watch for any hint of green on the brown countryside. The first brave little crocus signals it is time to work the land.

Prairie farmers will tell you that May is their favorite month. It is the beginning of a new crop year. Everywhere you look farmers are out in the field. Early pioneers were content to seed five acres a day. Nowadays, with modern equipment, farmers can seed more than 200 acres a day. But one thing has not changed. Each time a farmer plants a crop it is an act of faith. Faith that the rains will come, that the sun will shine and that the farmer will be there to harvest the best crop ever.

June is the greenest month, thanks to longer days of sunshine. These days are appreciated by farmers who have much work to do haying, crop spraying, fence fixing and summer-fallowing. But the long hot days are not appreciated by children stuck in school; they count the days until summer vacation. Teachers find it the perfect time for field trips.

July is the month for fairs. The rural community takes a break between "haying and harvest." When you think of a country fair, candy floss and midway rides come to mind, but it's also a time for good-spirited competition.

Our 4-H club members have been preparing for months to show off their skills in household arts and husbandry.

In August hot weather brings on harvest fast. You can smell the wheat ripening. Farmers work day and night to get their crops off, all the while keeping an eye on the sky for "the big White Combine" — hail clouds. A field hit by hailstones looks like a herd of elephants has stampeded through it. All the hard work can be wiped out in minutes.

In September with all the fall work to be done, one of the few distractions farmers allow themselves is an auction sale. The auctioneer's job is really recycling. He advertises to get people to the sale and then coaxes the very best price he can for the farmer client. Prices aren't set as in a store; each item is sold to the person who offers the most money. People come from miles around because it's entertaining as well as a great way to pick up a bargain.

October is the month for fall fowl suppers. They are an after-harvest tradition. Fowl suppers are held by various community groups as fund-raisers. Town populations swell when these suppers are held, as city folks often return to the communities they were raised in. But the children are busy preparing for another kind of party: October 31 — Halloween. What to wear?

November means it's time to head to Regina, Saskatchewan, for Agribition. People come from over thirty countries to see the best in agriculture and agribusiness. Ten thousand children come, to pet a buffalo, bid at an auction or watch a chick hatch. A popular exhibit lets them put their hands into bins of seed where they can feel real wheat, the slipperiness of flax or the tiny roundness of canola. Touring the cattle barns, they are quick to learn the "cow-pie two-step."

When we think of December we think of cold, snow and Christmas, as we on the prairies settle in for the winter. Communities organize special Christmas parties and concerts. Everyone is included. There is a feeling of peace and goodwill that makes us grateful and proud to call the prairies "home."

The Stubble Jumpers,

Jo and Yvette

To my son Matthew who enjoys every day of the year! — Jo
For my granddaughter Bailey, whose arrival made this year special. — Yvette

January

For Matthew, January means no sleeping in and no Saturday morning cartoons on television. Matthew is a hockey player but before he can join his teammates, chores must be done.

Wide-eyed cows watch as the family works in the quiet darkness of the frosty morning. The stillness is broken as Dad swings his axe, chopping at the thick ice that has filled in the cattle's dugout watering hole during the night. Mom delivers a mixture of wheat, oats, oyster shell and laying mash to the chickens. Matthew and his older brother pail oats into the feed trough. They finish off hauling hay bales. Dad drives while the boys heave the loaded bales off the tailgate of the pickup truck. By the time they finish, their eyebrows and the fronts of their tuques are coated with hoarfrost.

Soon the family is on its way but only as far as the local rink. There, they split up into car pools and go off to different tournaments. Every weekend it's different destinations.

When Matthew's team arrives at their tournament, the smell of frying onions greets them at the door. It smells wonderful. Volunteers have arrived long before to make sure the dressing rooms are unlocked, the ice scraped clean and grills turned on. People coming in make a beeline to the canteen counter. The success of a tournament relies heavily on the food. Rinks become known for their pierogi or pie, borscht or beef-on-a-bun.

Matthew suits up in the dressing room. It is crowded with kids, parents, coaches and equipment. Everyone is talking about last year when a chinook melted chunks of frost from the rink ceiling. It plopped down to the playing surface, landing on the players' helmets. One tiny but resourceful goalie collected the melted slush with his stick and formed a dike a few millimeters high in front of his net. It slowed down pucks and he almost had a shutout until the referee discovered it.

With the magic of skates, hockey tape and pads — shoulder pads, knee pads, neck pads, elbow pads, you-name-it pads — each child is transformed. They arrive as sleepy children and march out of the dressing room looking like gladiators.

You can begin to sense the excitement as you watch the teams warm up, each circling the ice sizing up the opposing team with a cool glance.

Matthew's coach huddles the team around the bench. There is only time for one last word of inspiring advice: "Remember, guys, those girls don't know we're afraid of them..."

January   At the rink children dream of playing in the big leagues

February

Craig loves a snowmobile poker derby. These snowmobile rallies on the prairies are organized as local fund-raisers but really they are just a good excuse for families to get together and have some winter fun.

When Craig and his dad arrive at the community hall, the parking lot is already filled up with cars and trucks and trailers. Snowmobilers dart around the new arrivals and make their way to the starting area. Zing! Zing! The sound of revving engines echoes in their ears. Craig is happy to see his school friends and his cousin Nicole have waited for him. Quickly he and his dad unload their sleds and go inside the hall to register. Already volunteers are in the kitchen serving coffee and doughnuts. Others are wrestling with the big copper vats out back. They are setting up for the pitchfork fondue. Riders are assured of a great supper on their return.

After signing in and paying the fees, each takes a first roll of the dice. Dad rolls a pair of fives.

"Not a bad start," says the volunteer who records the totals and initials Dad's card.

Craig rolls the dice hoping he might be the rider with the highest score after the five rolls and go home five hundred dollars richer.

"Snake eyes!" the man shouts and dutifully records a two on Craig's scorecard.

Dad and Craig suit up so they can begin their ride.

"People would be crazy to head out today not dressed properly," says Dad as he pulls on his balaclava and then his helmet over it. "You kids remember, this is not a race. Stay on the trail. I'll pull up the rear in case any of you have engine trouble."

It is the perfect day for a poker derby. You could get sunburned even though it is well below freezing. The sky is clear blue, the landscape is solid white. Craig is glad his helmet visor is tinted because the sun glare off the snow would be blinding.

Craig and his friends set out and the group has no difficulty following the well-traveled trail. They arrive at the first checkpoint: two trucks parked by a railroad crossing. This time Craig rolls another pair of snake eyes. The group hoots as another two is recorded on Craig's card.

The riders continue along the trail and make the designated stops. At Minard's Bluff, the dice are rolled and scores recorded. After, they warm up around the big bonfire with the other snowmobilers, and enjoy a roasted wiener and hot chocolate. Craig and his friends go back for seconds.

"Did you come to eat or to ride?" asks Dad.

On the way to the fourth stop, the trail leads past a big slough surrounded by buckbrush. Craig cannot resist the mounds of untouched snow on the far side, and he breaks away from the trail. His cousin Nicole follows. The two

February   Ice fishing and snowmobiling are a cure for winter doldrums

snowmobiles fly over drifts. It is exhilarating. They are startled when deer suddenly leap out of nowhere. Craig and Nicole bring their machines to an abrupt halt.

"Mulies!" Craig yells across the slough to the others, but they do not hear over their snowmobiles. Nicole and Craig watch the three mule deer run a short distance away and stop. The deer turn and stare back at them.

"They must have been hiding in the buckbrush," says Craig. "Boy, they're big. Probably the same ones getting fat feeding off our bale stack."

"Look at the size of their ears," says Nicole. "They're huge!"

The deer turn away as though they are insulted. They run across the prairie out of sight.

Both Craig and Nicole savor the moment. It is perfect.

It is not so perfect when they have to push their machines to get started in the deep powder. They catch up with the group waiting on the other side of the slough and continue their ride. Craig's luck with the dice does not improve. Not at the fourth checkpoint nor at the last stop, Uncle Fernand's fishing shack. Maybe the fishermen are having better luck but Craig is too distracted to ask them. His total score for the day is ten. To make matters worse, Craig's snowmobile refuses to start up when it comes time to return to the hall. He ends up being towed in.

By the time they arrive at the community hall, it is dark outside and Craig and his dad are cold and hungry. They are just in time. The crowd is about to sit down to eat.

Nicole and their friends have saved a place for them. The meal of potatoes and beans and rib-eye steak fondued on a pitchfork, tastes as good as it smells.

Prizes are handed out after dessert. It comes as no surprise when Mr. and Mrs. Yurkowski are called up to receive the prize for the oldest male and female drivers. It is the fourth year in a row they have won. They promise to return next year: "Even if they have to strap our wheelchairs to a snowmobile." Next, prizes go to the driver of the oldest machine, the driver who came from farthest away and the driver with the highest score. Nicole is disappointed to be only one number off winning the five hundred dollars. Craig is surprised when he is called up to the stage. The presenter hands Craig a check for twenty dollars — "For the lowest score" — then a trophy, and says, "Why if it wasn't for bad luck, Craig, you'd have no luck at all!"

March

There's an old expression "If March comes in like a lamb, it goes out like a lion."

A raging snowstorm woke the family that morning and sent Mom and Dad hurrying out with the four-wheel drive truck to round up the cows in the winter pasture. The cattle had been turned out because the weather had been very mild and it was much healthier for calves to be born on open range rather than in the winter feed lot where there was more risk of disease. It would take time to find and rescue all the newborn calves out in the fierce blizzard. Outside, the temperature was quickly dropping. There was not a minute to waste.

Dad's parting words were, "Jayme, you're in charge. Look after Michael. There's no school. The buses aren't running. And check on Jezebel. She might be ready to farrow. Remember, she's a gilt. It's her first litter — she could savage her young."

That's how Jayme and Michael ended up being midwives to a sow named Jezebel.

The children threw on yesterday's clothes and their work parkas and headed to the barn. As soon as they stepped out the door, the wind sucked away their breath. The yard was protected by a shelter belt, but they still had to walk leaning into the storm. By the time they reached the barn, their faces were wet and red from being pelted by the sleet-like snow.

Not wanting to excite the pregnant sow, they opened the door and stepped in quietly. Jayme found herself playing a game of tug-of-war with the wind when she tried to close the door. She finally won, slamming the door with a loud bang. Even after the door was latched, the wind still kept rattling it.

Jezebel was restless and panting. She was up and down, moving around in her stall. Romeo, the boar, stood peering over the concrete wall, looking like an anxious father. Finally Jezebel seemed to have the straw arranged to her liking and she nestled down.

"Michael, watch her but don't get too close," whispered Jayme. "I'll get the heat lamp and set up the litter pen."

Michael slid into the stall. "Jayme," he called softly, "Jayme, I think one's started to come out."

"I'm coming. Keep the piglets away from her head," ordered Jayme.

Jayme carried the portable lamp to the empty stall next to Jezebel's and rigged it up as fast as she could. She broke open a straw bale for bedding and spread it under the red warming lights, just as she had seen her father do many times. She wondered how she would manage if Jezebel were to go after her piglets or after Michael. How could she stop a three-hundred-pound sow?

A piglet let out a squeal.

"There's four of them. They're slippery. I can't hold them," Michael whined. He now lay sideways in the straw trying to corral four pink critters, using his body to make a barrier.

"Hand them over to me," Jayme whispered.

"I can't. They're too squirmy." Michael tried to hold onto one to prove it. The piglet squealed and wriggled out of Michael's hands. Romeo started snorting. Jezebel grunted and started rocking as if about to get up. Michael jumped up and onto the stall wall to get out of the way.

"Okay, Jezebel, it's okay," soothed Jayme. "Easy, girl."

The sow got up on her haunches and then flopped down on her opposite side. She managed to do it without landing on any of her babies. Out popped another piglet.

Michael threw up his hands and looked over at Jayme. "What do you want me to do?"

Then Jayme spied the solution. It was right there in front of them. "Michael, use the water pail!"

Michael grabbed the black rubber pail and emptied the water into the cement gutter. He scooped up the closest piglet and held the pail up to Jayme. She pulled it over and deposited the baby under the heat lamp. It happened so quickly the piglet didn't have time to protest. Jayme handed the pail back. They did it again and again. When they finished, twelve baby piglets were safely in the litter nest.

By the time Mom and Dad returned, Jayme had cleaned up Jezebel and settled her with the piglets. The sow's mothering instincts had come through and so had Michael's. He had fallen in love with the biggest of the litter and even named him Stormy.

March   Newborn piglets prove to be quite a handful

April

As he has done the second week of April for over fifty years, Grampa is busy preparing for some special guests — his chicks. For the first time, Tim is old enough to be his helper. The enclosed stall in the barn is cleaned out and all the cracks sealed. Next, a layer of fine sand is spread on the cement. They make sure there are no tiny stones the babies might choke on. Heat bulbs are checked and replaced, and the brooder lamp is rigged up just inches above the floor to provide the constant warmth the chicks will need.

Grampa fills the feeder pans and troughs with chick starter and Tim scrubs the water fountains and fills them with fresh drinking water.

"You'll keep these filled when I'm out in the field," says Grampa. "You'll be surprised how much they eat. Right away, too. They're smart. Not like turkeys — you have to practically stick their beaks in to show them how."

Soon all is ready — the perfect chick nursery, safe from hungry barn cats, skunks and rats.

On the trip home from the hatchery, Tim is happy he gets to hold the cardboard box full of chicks. He can hear them scratching and cheeping. He pokes his finger in through one of the air holes and feels their frantic pecking. It feels strange, like ticklish pinches.

"They think my finger is a big fat worm, Grampa," says Tim.

The first stop is at the house to show Gramma. Everyone marvels at the softness of the baby chicks. They feel like little balls of cotton. They are so new they still have their tiny egg tooth on the top of their little beaks.

As they scurry about already searching for food, it's hard to believe that they were just born earlier that day. By fall we will enjoy the fresh eggs they will provide.

Grampa says, "It's easier to buy eggs at the store but there's not the same satisfaction in it. Besides, ours taste better!"

April   Everyone marvels at the softness of the baby chicks

May

Leah has been recruited to help with planting the family garden. Today she helps Mom and Gramma plant potatoes. Gramma sits surrounded by pails and bags of old potatoes which she will cut in half with her favorite paring knife. She tosses the cut pieces into a smaller pail. Mom is busy digging the holes. Leah's job is to place the half slice of potato in the hole and then hill dirt over it.

"Make sure you put the potato eyes looking skyward," calls Gramma.

"I know how to do it, Gramma," says Leah. "I've already planted a pazillion potatoes."

"Not quite, dear," says Mom, "I count around two hundred. It leaves two hundred to go."

"Mom, did you know I hate planting potatoes?" says Leah as she slowly straightens up.

"Well, maybe what you need is a break," suggests Mom.

Leah perks up and thinks about escaping to the house away from the mosquitoes.

"How about you plant beans for a while," she continues. "You'll find the seeds over there by Gramma."

Leah's shoulders drop. "Can't we quit for a while?"

"If we quit now, Gramma and I will stiffen up and we'll never come back to finish. Go do beans. A change is as good as a rest."

Leah decides that planting beans has to be more fun than planting potatoes.

Gramma explains that beans must be planted in straight rows so Dad can rototill between them. She shows Leah how to use two stakes with a long string to make certain that she plants straight. Leah uses the string method for the first row and after that she just plants them helter-skelter. When Gramma sees what Leah is doing, she just smiles and says nothing.

Ten days later the women check the garden. Leah sees the results of her efforts for the first time. One straight outer row of beans stands in sharp contrast to a patch of crooked rows and scattered bean plants breaking through the soil.

"Can't rototill that patch, Leah," says Gramma. "You'll have to hoe. But," she adds with a smile, "you just may have found a way to fool the cutworms."

May   Learning to plant the family garden

June

Dan's class is going to dinosaur country. They leave the city early in the morning because they have a long drive ahead. Dan and his friends choose to sit at the back of the school bus. To stay cool, they have opened all the windows. It's like sitting in a wind tunnel. None of the teachers or parent chaperones sit at the back. The boys like it that way. The ride at the back is also a lot bumpier, so the boys hope that no one who gets "car sick" sits back there with them.

The first stop is Dinosaur Provincial Park. It is a surprise to travel through miles of green countryside and then suddenly descend into Alberta's badlands. The teacher explains that the park has been designated by the United Nations as a World Heritage Site because there is no place on earth quite like it. Dan agrees. The badlands are brown and gray, clay and rocks; wrinkled hills with stripes running crossways through them. These different colored stripes are layers of shale, coal, sandstone and mudstone. Scientists say these date back to the time just before the dinosaurs disappeared — sixty-five to seventy million years ago.

At the field station, the class meets the park interpreter who will be their guide. He explains that the station was established there because the paleontologists and technicians from the Royal Tyrrell Museum in Drumheller work in the park collecting fossils.

"There are two ways to collect fossils: surface collecting and excavating," says the park interpreter. "Surface collecting means finding isolated fossils lying on the ground. Excavating means digging out fossils embedded in the ground or rock. If you do this in the park without proper authorization and a permit, it is punishable by a fine or prison sentence."

Dan quickly forgets about taking any fossils home for a souvenir.

"The cottonwood trees growing along the river are endangered habitat. More than 95% of North America's riverside habitat has disappeared."

The group hikes uphill a short distance.

"We are going into the protected natural preserve. Here you will see what has been uncovered by fourteen thousand years of erosion. Two hundred million years ago, when dinosaurs roamed here, it was a swamp surrounded by lush plant growth. Now there is very little vegetation." He points to a small cactus blooming pink and yellow. "Please stay on the paths. Be watchful for rattlesnakes. Also, we have black widow spiders and a type of scorpion that can give a nasty sting."

Dan thinks their guide is just kidding, but as his classmates bombard the man with questions, he realizes there *are* rattlers and scorpions. Dan is glad to be wearing long pants and shoes instead of sandals.

At the first stop, the landscape is smooth clay hills. It is quite moon-like. Dan is first to spot what looks like a solid chunk of bone. It is as big as his fist. The

June   Before summmer vacation: a field trip to dinosaur country

interpreter tells him: "It's a vertebra, part of a dinosaur's spine — probably part of the tail." Dan cannot believe he is actually holding what was once part of a dinosaur's tail. Very quickly other students make finds as well: a tiny turtle shell, chunks of petrified wood and more bones. It is exciting. Soon they realize that you cannot move without stepping on a fossil, they are so plentiful. As the class moves on, Dan is glad that fossils can't be taken by souvenir hunters. This way someone else can "discover" them.

The next stop offers a spectacular view of the badlands from higher up. The whole class is quite in awe of this harsh landscape in front of them. It is beautiful. Then the interpreter takes them down into the valley. Halfway down the slope, they come across an actual dinosaur dig. An orange canvas secured by rocks covers the excavation. When the canvas covering is pulled back, an embedded skeleton in the hillside is revealed.

"This is an *Albertosaurus* or 'Alberta Lizard'," explains their guide. "It was the first dinosaur to be discovered by Joseph Tyrrell back in 1884. Since then over thirty-five species of dinosaur have been found in the park. The *Albertosaurus* was over eight meters long and weighed more than two tons. It was a fiercer hunter than its famous cousin, *Tyrannosaurus rex*."

As they journey further into the valley, they see the strangest sight yet. Hoodoos! Giant columns of sandstone with mushroom-like caps, sculpted over the centuries by wind, rain and running water. The interpreter tells them that Native people would never camp in the valley, only up on open prairie, because they believed these bizarre pillars were petrified giants who would come alive at night and throw down the cap rock at invaders. A

hundred years from now, these hoodoos may be gone, eroded by the weather. But they may disappear even faster because of vandalism and people touching them.

None of the class wants to leave when it is time to go. As the bus departs for the Royal Tyrrell Museum, their teacher reads a pamphlet to them: "It is one of the largest paleontological museums in the world. It displays more than two hundred dinosaur specimens, the largest number under one roof anywhere." The boys at the back of the bus do not hear a word. They are busy peering over a pamphlet Dan picked up at the Field Station.

"Experience the thrill of unearthing fossils for scientific research. Come with us on a real dinosaur dig," it reads.

Dan hopes his parents will let him return during the summer holidays. And maybe someday he will become a real paleontologist.

July

Marla is entered in the 4-H Beef competition. She is the fourth generation of her family to show cattle at the local fair. She has entered several classes with her heifer, Pansy, and her steer, Rolf.

For the first two days of the fair, she will be too busy to even think about candy floss or the midway. That's just fine with her. She's been thinking about the competition since last year's fair and preparing for it since last fall when she picked out her two calves.

Last year when she was in the ring with her steer, it broke loose from her grasp and jumped over the barriers. It was very embarrassing and she has vowed it won't happen again.

How does an eighty-pound girl keep a 1000-pound steer from leaping out of a show ring?

Marla has worked with her calves for ten months. First she halter-broke them. Then she practiced leading them around and posing them. The leading didn't take long to learn but teaching them to pose properly required a lot more time and patience. After that, she ran the calves through the paces just often enough so they wouldn't forget their training. She had her calves ready for the ring this year.

The whole family moves in onto the fairgrounds the day before. The cattle are settled in the fair barns and all the necessary equipment and feed has been unloaded. It's hard work getting around all the other bodies doing the same thing, not to mention the people who have come to the Scotsman's fair ahead of time so they won't have to pay admission.

Next, they set up their tent in the 4-H village located in the center of the fairground racetrack. Marla's younger brother bemoans the fact that they don't have a fancy RV like other people. "It would be so much easier just to park it and turn on the television and the air conditioning."

Marla knows exactly what her father will say. She has heard it a hundred times before: "Maybe next year, Jeff, if there's a crop." Then he tells them that when he was in 4-H his family stretched a canvas over the back of a grain truck for shelter.

4-H families visit back and forth as they get set up. Soon members from thirteen different clubs are settled in the village. Renewing friendships and making new ones is the best part of the fair.

It rains during the night and the fairgrounds become a sea of mud. Marla is downright owly.

"It's unfair. Why does it always rain at fair time? How can I keep my calves clean and ready for show?"

"Marla, it's rained on everybody," Dad reminds.

Rolf's up first and off to the wash rack to be shampooed and rinsed. Once he is installed in the grooming rack, he is blow-dried and brushed and moussed and curled and trimmed. Hooves are polished and his tail teased into a puff ball. Marla does everything just as she practiced.

Soon it is show time!

Marla throws on her 4-H club jacket and leads Rolf over to the show barn, praying that neither of them slips in the mud on the way.

As she enters and circles the ring, Marla sees that she and Rolf are up against some tough competition. Ten 4-H'ers and their steers compete in front of a full house. The audience is made up of family and friends and future bidders for the final sale after the competition is over.

Marla does not look forward to the big sale when Rolf will go to the highest bidder. She knows the money she receives will go into the bank for her college fund but it's tough to part with an animal you've worked with for over a year. She is glad the rules allow her to keep her heifer, Pansy.

The judge indicates he wishes them to pose their steers now. One boy has trouble with his calf. It balks and rears and bangs into its neighbors.

Marla strokes Rolf with her show cane and talks to him. He responds beautifully and Marla relaxes and enjoys showing him. The judge walks around checking each animal over for its confirmation. He indicates to Marla to line up first. The rest are lined up after her. She is happy when her name is announced over the loudspeaker: "Marla May, first place!"

As she poses for a photo with Rolf, Marla has a good feeling about this fair. Maybe — just maybe — she'll win the showmanship class or have a grand champion.

But she does not have much time to daydream. She has to get Pansy ready.

July   For the 4-H Beef competition each calf is groomed to perfection

August

August means the start of harvest. Sarah loves harvest. It's the way her parents earn a living but it's more than that. It's the way the whole family works together and everyone has a job, whether you're big or little.

Sarah likes working with her Grampa Raymond best, hauling grain. The other adults always seem to be in a big hurry, but Grampa Raymond gets the job done at his own speed. If they are sitting in the truck waiting for a load, he takes time to point out different birds. Or they hop out of the truck and hunt for arrowheads. And Grampa Raymond always has time to answer her questions:

"How do you know when the wheat is ready?"

Grampa Raymond hopped down from the big grain truck. "Come, I'll show you."

He bent down over the windrowed straw and picked out a missed wheat stem. He rubbed the head of the wheat in his hand. Out came tiny brown kernels. He blew the tiny husks of chaff away. Picking out a single kernel, he handed it to Sarah.

"Bite it," he said. He put a kernel between his teeth and bit down. "Hear the crack sound when you bite? That means it's ready."

Sarah nodded her head. She heard it.

Grampa Raymond handed her more kernels. "Chew on them. When I was a kid, this was our gum."

Sarah chewed. It tasted like old flavorless gum.

"Good crop on this field. Number one wheat. Makes the best flour," Grampa Raymond explains.

"Grampa," a voice calls from the truck box. Suddenly up pops Sarah's cousins, Luke and Aaron. They have been "swimming" in the grain.

"I lost my shoe," said Luke.

"Well, you'd better find it quick. Sarah's mom will be wanting us to pick up another load soon," said Grampa Raymond pointing to the combine.

Down went the two heads into the truck box.

Sarah smiled as she remembered doing the same thing last year. She guessed it was a harvest tradition — just like meals in the field and learning to drive the grain truck when you're big enough so you can reach the gas pedal and still see over the dashboard.

August   Grampa explains how to tell when the wheat is ready for harvest

September

Alix's dad is an auctioneer. He's a farmer too but like many prairie farmers he has another job. He says he needs it "so he can afford to farm!" He works for his mom and dad who run an auction business.

After he graduated from high school, he went to auctioneer school and it turns out he has a real talent for the business. People say, "He can sell a floor polisher to a woman with wall-to-wall carpet!" Alix hopes that she has the same talent so she can go to auctioneer school, too. Dad likes the idea of three generations in the business.

Even now, Alix is given a job. She is a marker. She stands by or on the piece of machinery, holding the red marker so that the crowd knows for sure what is up for bid.

Once when she was holding the marker at a sale she saw something strange. A tiny little house over by the trees seemed to move from side to side. The people in front of her didn't notice because they had their backs to it. Grampa and Dad didn't see it because they were working hard hustling bids.

Then the moving stopped. Alix thought she must be seeing things. The bidding got serious and she got busy watching the bidders. When the bidding was finished, they moved down to the next piece of machinery.

Perched up on the seat of the old Case tractor, Alix saw the little shack move again. It rocked a bit. Now she was sure it moved. She slid down, walked over to her dad and yanked at his pant leg. Dad paid no attention but Alix persisted until he was so distracted by her tugging that it threw him off his calling.

He bent down. "What is it, Alix?" he said into the microphone.

"Daddy, that little house over there is moving." She pointed. Everyone heard her over the loudspeaker and turned to look. Sure enough, the little house was gently rocking.

"It's the outhouse," said a voice in the crowd.

"Maybe someone's stuck inside," said another voice.

It turned out that the ground was soft from the rain that had fallen the previous day and when a rather large woman went in, it had sunk so the door jammed into the dirt and couldn't be opened. No one had heard her calls for help because of the PA system.

Everyone had a good laugh and the woman was embarrassed but grateful to be set free.

Just goes to show, you never know what will happen at an auction.

September   A farm auction offers entertainment as well as a bargain

October

For children, Halloween is the most exciting event during October. It means dressing up in costumes and going from house to house trick-or-treating.

But Halloween is different for rural children. Because of the great distances between farms and ranches, children cannot walk from house to house. A parent or older sibling must drive the young ones. Often the "chauffeurs" join in the fun and get dressed up too. Don't be surprised if you happen to see Frankenstein or an ugly old witch driving a pickup truck.

The great distances also mean that farm folk don't see as many trick-or-treaters. Because of this, they tend to be overly generous with treats and money. It's their way of thanking the children for coming to visit. Half a dozen stops can fill a UNICEF box and a candy sack equal to a whole night's trick-or-treating in the city.

For Torry and Tyler, the bus ride home after school seems to take forever. The Halloween party at school has whet their appetite for trick-or-treating. As soon as the school bus drops them off, they race to get their few chores done. They make sure that their carved jack-o'-lanterns are set out so they will be seen. They sneak a few treats their mother has set out — "Just testing, to make sure they're not poisoned," they say when she catches them.

Both boys hardly touch their supper. They are too busy planning their visitation route.

Soon, it will be nightfall; time for ghosts and goblins to go out to play. Tyler and Torry beg to get an early start. They hurry to get dressed up. This year they have decided to go as monsters. Dad, if anyone asks, is a cowboy.

After checking to see no eggs are missing from the fridge, Mom allows her "men" to go. She stays home to hand out candy and to be on the lookout for any tricksters with eggs or soap. Last year, someone soaped the windows. It was hard work to scrub it off. Mom figures it was cousin Wes and she's still trying to think of a way to get even.

The first stop is always Auntie Marilyn's. She makes the best caramel popcorn balls. Uncle Bobo will have a surprise. He is a trickster. One year the boys found him on his porch propped up in a coffin box. It was great. Everyone took a turn climbing into the coffin to pose for a photo. Last year he served them a tray of dead flies and chocolate-covered grasshoppers.

The boys wonder what he has in store for them this year.

October   On Halloween ghosts and goblins travel by pickup truck

November

Jared loves Agribition almost as much as he loves Clydesdale horses. He is the fifth generation of the family to be working with the big Clydes and he was only four years old when he was leading these gentle giants to the show ring at Agribition.

Last year, he turned nine and was finally old enough to enter the Junior Showmanship Halter class. This year, he hopes that Dad and Uncle Bill will let him enter the Junior Hitch class. Back in July when the entry forms arrived, the men started to plan which of their forty horses they would take to Agribition. Jared suggested that maybe he could enter the hitch class. One of the men said "maybe." That's how Jared came to be living on a "maybe" for five months.

All that time, he has practiced for his halter class and at every opportunity he drove the chore team. But Jared's dream was not to drive a chore team. He wanted to drive someone else's team in the show ring — Mr. Gordeyko's. Jared felt he had the finest hitch team in the country.

Five months isn't really long but if you're living on a "maybe," it can seem forever. And when they get to Agribition, Dad and Uncle Bill don't even remember saying "maybe."

"No, you're only ten," said Dad.

Uncle Bill said, "You're not ready. Maybe next year."

Mr. Gordeyko said, "My team is very spirited. They love to be in the ring. It takes all my strength to hold them." Jared knows in his heart they are right, but he is disappointed.

Then Mr. Gordeyko suggests, "Perhaps you could ride with me. You know the rules. I need an assistant driver. It will be good experience for you."

Jared did not need to be asked twice.

When it came time for the hitch class, Jared was up on the wagon before the horses were hitched. As the teams rumbled into the show ring, it was all Jared could do just to hold onto his seat. He gripped tightly onto the rail guard.

All the teams were magnificent but none stepped as lively around the ring as the Gordeyko team. It came as no surprise when the judge presented them with first prize. Jared held the prize ribbon high as they made their victory circle around the show ring.

Jared knew that his time would come to drive a team in the ring and someday it would even be a six team hitch — no "maybe's" about it.

November   At Agribition lucky is the child allowed to ride with a winning team

December

Everyone in the community is busy preparing for the Christmas holiday. The volunteer fire department strings up Christmas lights across the main street. Moms are busy cleaning house, decorating, baking and shopping. Gifts are wrapped; parcels and cards are mailed to those who won't be there for the holiday. Dads are sent out with strict orders to "Bring home a straight Christmas tree this year!"

The children stage the Christmas concert. Every child is assigned a role. The seven-year-olds get to do the Nativity story. Rynette is an angel; her younger sister, Chantelle, is a member of the Suzy Snowflake chorus line. Both girls are happy; they practice for days in front of the mirror and get to wear gold tinsel in their hair.

When the big night arrives, the entire main street is lined with cars and trucks. It is standing room only inside the community hall. No one wants to miss the show. The audience is made up of friends and family.

There is a special sense of expectancy in the air. The children are excited about having their turn on stage. This year the concert is not much different from last year, or the year before. The only thing that changes is the children. Some children may be in the same role their parents performed when they were small.

The children know the concert is over when the piano starts to play "Here Comes Santa Claus," and Santa Claus bursts through the front door. He hands out a small gift, calling each child by name.

Chantelle is afraid to go forward but Rynette steps up and holds her by the hand. Together they get their presents. Soon Santa's work is done and he vanishes out through the door.

That's when Chantelle realizes that she has not thanked Santa for her present. She races to the door and sticks out her head. She is surprised to see Santa Claus pulling away in a red pickup truck. The truck moves down Main Street and turns out of sight at the grain elevator.

Later when the girls are getting ready for bed, Chantelle tells Rynette what she saw. "He didn't have a sleigh and reindeer. He was in a red truck."

"Of course," said Rynette in her big sister I-know-everything voice. "He wasn't really Santa Claus."

Chantelle is stunned by Rynette's pronouncement.

"The real Santa Claus is at the North Pole working. He can't go to every Christmas concert," Rynette continues.

Chantelle perks up. "Of course," she thinks, very relieved. "Of course."

"It has to be someone from around here, though," Rynette said confidently, "because he knew our names."

The girls stare into the night wondering, "Who was the Santa Claus?"

December The girls stare into the night and wonder about Santa Claus

Glossary

borscht - a soup made with beets

chinook - a warm wind that blows from the Pacific Ocean across the Rocky Mountains and sweeps across the prairies

confirmation - physical characteristics of the animal breed

cutworm - a caterpillar that cuts off the stalks of young plants near or below the ground

egg tooth - a tiny sharp point on the top of a beak, used by the bird to crack open its shell to hatch

farrow - give birth to a litter of pigs

4-H - a farm club where children learn agriculture and home economics. The objective is the improvement of head, heart, hands and health.

gilt - a sow that has not yet had a litter of pigs

hatchery - a commercial operation that hatches eggs

heifer - a young cow that has not yet had a calf

husbandry - farming skills

paleontologist - a scientist who collects and studies fossils

pierogi - tiny dumplings filled with potato, cheese or meat

pitchfork fondue - steaks, roasts and other food skewered on a large haying fork and dipped to cook in vats of hot oil

slough - a body of water formed by rain or melted snow in a natural depression in the land

steer - a castrated male calf

summer fallow - land worked in the summer but not seeded

windrow - a row of hay or straw raked together to make it easier to pick up later

© 1994 Jo Bannatyne-Cugnet: text
© 1994 Yvette Moore: art
Published in Canada by Tundra Books, Montreal, Quebec H3Z 2N2
Published in the United States by Tundra Books of Northern New York, Plattsburgh, N.Y. 12901
Library of Congress Catalog Number: 93-61792

Canadian Cataloging in Publication Data:
Bannatyne-Cugnet, Jo
    A Prairie Year
ISBN 0-88776-334-0 (hardcover) 10 9 8 7 6 5 4 3 2 1
    1. Farm life-Prairie Provinces-Juvenile literature. I. Moore, Yvette II. Title.
PS8553.A587P73 1994 j630'.9712 C94-900044-2 PZ7.B36Pr 1994

Design by Dan O'Leary
Transparencies by Jim Shipley
Printed in Canada by DW Freisen